T0353800

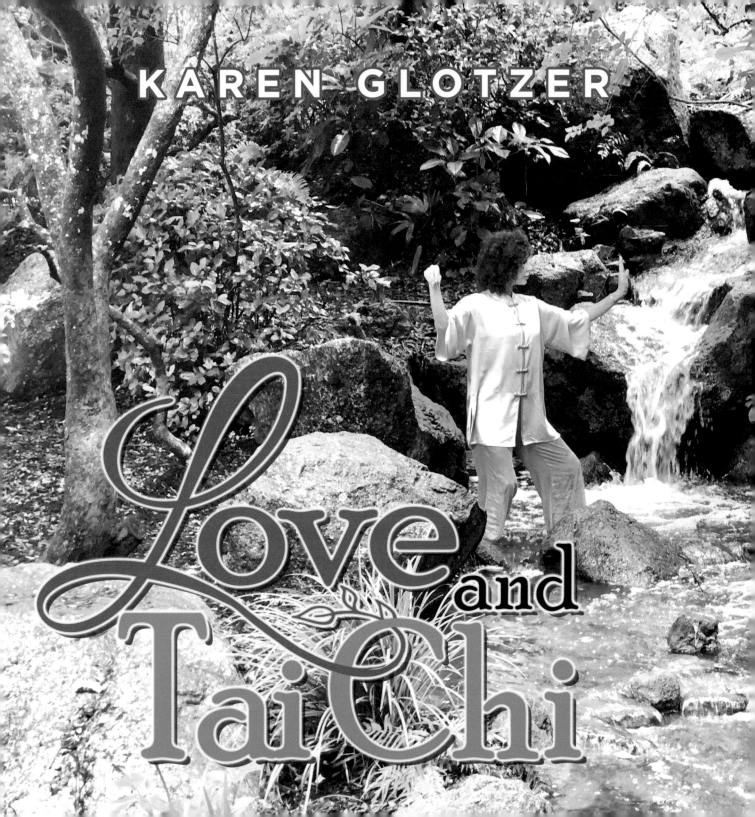

KAREN GLOTZER

Love and TaiChi

LOVE AND TAI CHI

Copyright © 2018 Karen Glotzer.

All rights reserved. No part of this book may be used or reproduced by any means, graphic, electronic, or mechanical, including photocopying, recording, taping or by any information storage retrieval system without the written permission of the author except in the case of brief quotations embodied in critical articles and reviews.

iUniverse books may be ordered through booksellers or by contacting:

iUniverse
1663 Liberty Drive
Bloomington, IN 47403
www.iuniverse.com
1-800-Authors (1-800-288-4677)

Because of the dynamic nature of the Internet, any web addresses or links contained in this book may have changed since publication and may no longer be valid. The views expressed in this work are solely those of the author and do not necessarily reflect the views of the publisher, and the publisher hereby disclaims any responsibility for them.

Any people depicted in stock imagery provided by Getty Images are models, and such images are being used for illustrative purposes only.
Certain stock imagery © Getty Images.

ISBN: 978-1-5320-5822-6 (sc)
ISBN: 978-1-5320-5823-3 (e)

Library of Congress Control Number: 2018911263

Print information available on the last page.

iUniverse rev. date: 10/12/2018

Love and Tai Chi

by
Karen L. Glotzer

A FAMILY PUSHES TOGETHER

Table of Contents

Gratitude

"Karen has truly embraced her journey in the practice and beauty of tai chi both externally and internally. It has been a pleasure to watch her develop from a beginning player to a dedicated student of the art."

Sifu Linda Morrissey - elitechinesemartialarts.com - Rockland County, New York

"Karen Glotzer is a dedicated tai chi student and poet. She consistently practices the principles of harmony; expressing herself poetically with calmness, patience and balance. She is a poet at heart, and tai chi is poetry in motion; an expression of one's true self."

Sifu Gary Tong – atouchofchi.com - Palm Beach County, Florida

"Karen Glotzer is a true Taiji poet. Her works bring much to the table for one to contemplate. Karen's poems are as descriptive as a video in your mind. I personally like them very much. We will be featuring her poetry from time to time in our new IAM Online Magazine oI Internal Arts.

John P. Painter - PhD, ND The Gompa Center www.thegompa.com - Arlington, Texas

"In the 25 years I have been studying Taiji, Karen still remains one of the most enthusiastic and inspired Taiji practitioners. Her inspiration transcends Tai Chi and extends into the realm of poetry. Karen has managed to unite poetry and posture in a manner that honors yin and yang while adding value to both.

Sifu Edmund Durso – The Fire Mountain School of Resilient Stress Management and Chinese Martial Arts thefiremountainschool.com - Nyack, New York

BRUSH KNEE AND PUNCH DOWN AND
RIGHT FOOT KICKS TO SIDE

Introduction

The graceful, balanced movements of tai chi can be compared to the rhyme and rhythm of poetry. In fact, tai chi is poetry in motion. It is an amazing, pleasurable form of exercise that has an ethereal quality. As you become more and more proficient, you fall in love with the movement itself.

In my previous book, <u>Emotional Explosions,</u> published in 2016, I tried to keep the poems accessible to everyone. I often included "author's notes" to aid the reader's comprehension. In <u>Love and Tai Chi,</u> I again concentrate on clarity and simplicity, with inclusion of author's notes. (I wish T. S. Elliot had done the same. It would have made grad school easier.) Because there are references to the poetic names of tai chi postures, I include them as well. Along with the poetry are ordinary pictures of mostly ordinary people doing the 37 tai chi postures of the Yang form. Just about anyone can learn and love tai chi.

My poems answer questions for anyone who would like to know what tai chi is all about. They provide an inspiration to learn tai chi, not instructions about how to do the forms. For actually learning the art, one must seek a good teacher. The reader will learn that tai chi is relatively easy to do, because it does not require great strength or difficult body postures. The book answers questions such as what is tai chi, why practice tai chi, what does tai chi look like, what is the philosophy of tai chi, and how does it apply to everyday life? The reader also learns about the mysterious "chi" or "qi" that is part of the word "tai chi," or "taiji" itself.

Many of my poems do not mention tai chi at all. That is because I incorporate the principles of tai chi into multi-faceted subjects. I write of romance, friendship, animals, love, loss, martial artists, and many other topics. The reader will learn that tai chi is also a martial art. The name "tai chi" actually means "Grand Ultimate Fist."

Love and Tai Chi is also a story of my personal journey to learn tai chi, a process that continues, because there is always something new to discover. Besides the physical benefits (balance, relaxation, flexibility, strength, energy), tai chi is a form of meditation. The meditation is done standing so it is great as a weight bearing exercise as well. It is also an exercise that relies heavily upon brain use. Yes! Thinking is required. Perhaps it is best stated in _The Harvard Medical School Guide to Tai Chi_ by Dr. Peter M. Wayne and Mark Fuerst, "Tai Chi training integrates slow, intentional movements with breathing and cognitive skills (for example, mindfulness and imagery). It aims to strengthen, relax, and integrate the physical body and mind." (Wayne and Fuerst, pg. 14) My poems support many of the principles stated in this very important book.

Tai Chi is especially useful as we age. Twenty years ago, when I began my tai chi practice, I had no idea that my left shoulder was slowly being eaten away by arthritis. Today the doctors I have seen are amazed by my range of motion. Therefore, I do not need replacement surgery yet, and I hope to never do it.

In summation, if you want to move like water as it slowly coils its way down the stream, or feel like you are walking upon clouds; learn tai chi. If you would like to feel like a tree, standing steady and strong so that gusts of wind can't knock you down; learn tai chi. Read my book and learn tai chi. Perhaps you, too, will fall in love with the movement.

SEPARATION OF RIGHT FOOT

WAVE HANDS LIKE CLOUDS

Thirty-seven Yang Form Postures

1. Commencement
2. Ward Off Left
3. Roll Back
4. Press Forward
5. Push
6. Single Whip
7. Raise Hands
8. Shoulder Stroke
9. White Crane Spreads Her Wings
10. Brush Knee and Twist
11. Deflect Downwards, Parry and Punch
12. Apparent Close
13. Cross Hands
14. Carry Tiger to Mountain
15. Fist Under Elbow
16. Repulse Monkey
17. Slantingly Flying /Part Wild Horse's Mane
18. Needle at Sea Bottom
19. Fan Through Back
20. Turn and Chop With Fist
21. Wave Hands Like Clouds
22. High Pat on Horse
23. Separation of Right or Left Foot
24. Kick With Sole
25. Brush Knee Punch Downward
26. Right Ft Kicks Upward
27. Hit Tiger
28. Right Foot Kicks Up and Side
29. Fair Lady Works the Shuttles
30. Snake Creeps Down
31. Golden Rooster Stands on One Leg
32. Cross Palms and Thrust
33. Turn and Kick, Scissors Step
34. Step Up to Form 7 Stars
35. Retreat to Ride Tiger
36. Lotus Kick
37. Shoot Tiger With Bow

First Glimpse

In the arms of old men
You are not diminished.
Graceful as white cranes above,
On a gray March morning,
You stir the Suzhou air.
In this strange eastern city,
Where the ten thousands
Rush by on bikes,
You remain rooted, soft,
Poised, balanced,
Preserved through time,
Movement in perfect rhyme!

I did not expect such beauty
From the arms of old men.

I press my head against the window.
My eyes close against the pain.

This was one of my first tai chi poems. It is about my first glimpse of tai chi, on a visit to China. I was in a hotel, and the sun had just risen. Down beneath my window I saw a group of older men performing a lovely routine that consisted of graceful, smooth movements. It looked like a wonderful, gentle exercise.

The Magic of the Tai Chi Energy Ball

Stand firmly with your legs apart,
Feel the beating of your heart.
Knees may be just slightly bent,
Relaxing is your first intent.
Root your legs just like a tree.
You'll learn to fill with energy.
A strong wind will not knock you down.
Your balanced stance will keep you strong.

Imagine that you hold a ball.
A common practice of tai chi,
The ball is one you cannot see.
But you will feel its buoyancy,
Like air, like wind, it's mystery.

Felt between your facing palms,
A jolt of electricity,
You stand, you breathe, you feel amazed,
Your inner sun begins to blaze.
Let the world go on its way,
You've nothing else to do today.

Just breathe and feel the energy,
This force is what is called your chi.
It builds between your open palms,
A golden light shines from your arms.

Do not let your spine be slack,
Push the ball, roll it back,
Keep the elbows slightly bent,
A circular path is your intent.

Breathe and feel the energy.
You're learning how to move your chi.
Around a circle you will go,
Like a turtle, very slow,
As you stand upon the ground,
As you move your ball around,
The light that comes from heaven's glow,
Brings harmony to those below.

I Swim in Morning Air

I swim in morning air
Yet I've roots deep in the earth.
My strokes are the branches
Of trees that sway from gentle wind,
Still I'm rounded as the Buddha.

I breathe the morning air,
And my breaths are one with the surf.
My arms are the wings
Of birds that sail with gentle breezes,
Still I'm proud to be the tiger.

I glide through morning air,
And my dance is my protection.
My art has sprung from
Dynasties past,
And we blend into the future.

I'm the swirling autumn leaf
That twirls, sails, rocks, sways-
Then gently floats
Upon the water.

HIGH PAT ON HORSE

Why

Your balance improves the most of all.
For youth and health, you'll hold the key.
As you age you'll never fall,
So come and learn tai chi with me.

Watch the crazy world rush by,
While you retain tranquility.
With calmness you can concentrate.
Please come and learn tai chi with me.

You'll fall in love with movements slow,
While cultivating energy.
You'll love the meditative forms,
So come with me and learn tai chi.

Watch the master in the park,
He seems to float above the breeze.
More graceful than a gliding crane,
So come with me and learn tai chi.

A book that came from Harvard Med,
Will prove increased immunity,
From shingles, colds and cancer too,
For those who learn and play tai chi.

And if you still are unconvinced,
It's even great for pregnancy.
You'll feel a deep serenity,
So come and learn tai chi with me.

WARD OFF LEFT

Touched by Tai Chi

For Sifu Gary Tong

Those passing by viewed a breathtaking dance,
Performed to the music of nature's sounds.
Delicate grace deserves more than a glance.
My senses perceived him float above ground.

Strong arms spread out like the crane's wings for flight,
Then he changed - a tiger ready to fight!
His postures were notes I wished I could sing,
With harmony soothing harsh morning's light.

The forms he performed as I watched intrigued,
Flowed gently like water drifting downstream.
As his loose clothes swirled in the gentle breeze,
His enlightened face was bewitching to see.

My mind and body were touched by tai chi.
I captured its spirit in poetry.

Author's note - Some of my poems are expressions of gratitude to my teachers, fellow students, martial art movie stars, and others who helped me learn about tai chi. Occasionally I made an effort to copy Shakespeare's sonnet form.

ROOSTER STANDS ON ONE LEG

ROOSTER STANDS ON ONE LEG

3 FEMALE ROOSTERS

LOTUS KICK

RIGHT FOOT KICKS UPWARD

MANY TAI CHI POSTURES HAVE NAMES THAT REFER TO ACTIONS WITH TIGERS. THESE MOVES REPRESENT "CARRY TIGER TO THE MOUNTAIN" AND "RIDE THE TIGER."

Meditation

Tai chi looks peaceful and easy to do
It calms your body and spirit as well.
With movements slow and gentle too,
Your very first lesson proves this to be true.

You learn the moves that the Chinese perform
To cultivate harmony of body and mind,
They meet by the pond where the lotus plants grow,
Appearing each morning at the same time.

As you learn balance with awesome skill,
Deep questions will form and flow through your mind,
You'll learn an awareness like never before,
And though the world's rushing, you can unwind.

Tai chi is also a martial art; circle the ball, step to your right
Some say it's the PhD of defense
As you coil your body; and keep your thighs tight,
You'll soon learn these movements will teach you to fight.

What is Tai Chi

How does one define tai chi?
It's really a philosophy;
That teaches balance, yin and yang,
That's based on nature's harmony.

Seek a place where pine trees grow,
Then firmly stand upon the ground.
Be a tree in sunlight's glow,
Withstand the wind; its gusty blow.
Your feet are roots just like the tree's
Your head seeks sun like flowers do,
Between the earth and sky you stand,
As sun's warmth pours itself through you.
Your hands and mouth help chi to flow,
As you stand grounded on the land.
You're activating energy,
And now you start to understand.

There are secrets hidden in tai chi.
It is more than healthy exercise.
For martial use, it's Ph.D.
Those who practice are the wise.

Bagua, Memory of 9/11/2001

The stillness of the morning
The common autumn sounds,
Are chirping birds and buzzing bees,
And acorns dropping to the ground.

We've come to walk in circles,
And fight a phantom foe,
Whirling bodies in the wind,
Seeking balance as we go.

Puzzled sparrows perched above us,
Watch from branches as we pass.
How curious are these humans,
Pounding rings upon the grass!

Our battle's fought with honor.
Face to face the weapon's plain.
And when things fall from sky to earth
It's only drops of rain.

And the river shines like metal,
Sparkles silver as we play;
Not yet hinting of the dragon's
Devastation down the way.

If a mountain can't stop thunder,
And lightning causes flame,
If towers crumble to the earth,
How do we bear such pain?
How do we bear such pain?

By spinning, sweeping, bending,
We fight a foe named grief,
With hope an autumn morning,
Will help us find relief.

So here we walk in circles,
And fight a phantom foe,
Whirling bodies in the wind,
Seeking balance as we go.

*Author's Note: This poem is about a lovely, advanced form of tai chi called bagua. It consists of choreographed combat routines which are performed in a circle. The postures contain applications for attack and self defense. We practiced on the soft grass of Memorial Park in Nyack, NY. Thus we pounded "rings upon the grass." The park is located along the Hudson River, approximately 25 miles north of the Twin Towers, where the 9-11 terrorist attack occurred, minutes before we began our practice. I kept the language simple as a *contrast to the horrible action. The five elements that are important to Chinese philosophy are in this poem as well: water, mountain, metal, earth, fire.*

NEEDLE AT SEA BOTTOM

Doctor John Painter's Lesson

From staring at a tree,
From walking in a circle,
A sick child regained his health.

Years later, the grown up man
Would become a renowned Sifu*
Who could capture an audience like a super-star,
As he stood among poles like imitation trees.
That were placed in precise positions.

We all love ghost stories,
So the charismatic man told us one.
He said he was a weak, sickly kid who one night
Saw a ghost outside his window.
It was a spinning white cloud.
With terrifying hands
That seemed to strike invisible prey.
The weak boy hid under his blanket,
Like a scared cat,
Not daring to peak out again.

"No ghost," his father said the next day.
"It's our new neighbor, a Chinese man.
I don't know what he is doing,
But I see him walking in circles in the night.
Among the trees."

"Come walk in circles with me my young friend,"
Spoke the Chinese man to the fragile boy, the next day.
"I will teach you to be still as water without wind,
And free from the illnesses
That plague the poor human body.
Of course, first you must stare at a tree."

The child's mind was as open as the sky,
Which fills with light each morning.
Being non-judgmental, he followed the Chinese man.
He was told to stand in front of a tree,
A pine tree with roots sturdy and deep,
And hold out his arms like an embrace.
This was how the lesson began.
Be like the tree. Don't move.
Be still; Be calm; Be strong.
Then walk in a circle for one hour a day.

The child grew wiser and stronger, like a tree unruffled by gusty winds.
The illnesses that plagued his young body
Began to retreat.
His powerful qi pushed them away
Like fresh water washes away waste.
He learned to become whole like a circle,
And then to become a skilled teacher.
Who would help others with what he had learned,
From staring at a tree.
From walking in a circle.

*Sifu - master teacher

Author's Note - Dr. John Painter is an expert on Jiulong, Baguazhang, Taijiquan, and Xingyiguan from the Li family's system. I had the pleasure of attending his presentation that was given at Master Jou's Centennial Celebration in July 2017. This poem explains how Dr. Painter became healthy after much illness as a child. He was fortunate to have Master Li Longdau as a neighbor in Texas, who took an interest in him. His training with Master Li, not only cured him, but led him to become an honored humanitarian through his works in martial, internal arts, and healing. It was indeed an honor to meet him. Later, I learned that he was a trained actor as well. I thought his stage presence was amazing. He directs a wonderful martial arts school in Arlington Texas, called The Gompa. He is a super-star.

Dragon Eats Sun

A golden sword of light
Pierced the sky as the purple sun arose from the sea.
It seemed to throw a disk at me.
I thought of light and energy,
Then recalled a distant memory
Of the time I'd taken LSD.
Amazingly,
Outside the yellow circle
A blue ring became a perimeter for the sun.
A holy shape appeared
That shimmered in white like a deity.
Then faded out and was done.

Blue spikes threw themselves at the circle,
As if a huge sea urchin was attempting to keep the sun apart.
Then the sun began to pulsate in sync with my beating heart.
A miracle occurred when the sun split into two suns
Which bounced around like dots.
Who appeared to do battle for placement.
Then one vanished
And reappeared in a different spot,
Only to vanish again.

Finally I closed my eyes as one tear slowly fell down my face,
Perhaps from the wind?
Or perhaps I felt a memory,
From a place I'd never been?

What had primitive man thought
While watching suns rise in the past?
With his lack of science and more
Did he think he'd seen God at last.

I wished my cold hands,
Might have warmed from the sun,
But the beach was still cold,
And the magic was done.

*Author's Note- This was an exercise performed at dawn on a beach in Florida. It was incredible to actually hallucinate while staring at the sun. Someone who is educated in this practice needs to lead, because the sun can damage the eye. Taking LSD in my youth was scary. It is not a good idea.

REPULSE THE MONKEY AND CROSS PALMS AND THRUST

Sonnet to Jet Li

He moves like a poem with meter and form,
The tai chi master of motion and grace.
Like a snake winds through **driftwood** *to seek prey,*
His strike is **steel** *if the force hits your face.*
Eyes slantingly upwards, smile of boy,
He darkens when grasping bird's tail in the sun.
Single whips shatter **rocks;** *gold dust falls to* **earth***,*
Black hair shakes loose from his faji, his bun.
Circular power, released energy;
He becomes the white crane lifting to **sea***.*
What strength is such to defy gravity!
I've captured his beauty in poetry!

I dreamed of a mirror where yang became yin.
Minds and bodies combined—
His to mine, mine to him.

Author's Note: I loved his film **Tai Chi Master.** *I include the five elements important to Chinese philosophy in this poem, and I refer to tai chi forms: Grasping the Bird's Tail, Slantingly Upwards, Single Whip, White Crane Spreads Her Wings*

A WHITE CRANE WHO IS NOT YET SPREADING ITS WINGS

WHITE CRANE SPREADS ITS WINGS

What is the Black White Circle Thing

My friend asked me a question,
That I wished to answer clearly.
But like a wait at DMV,
Our time was used up nearly.

She'd asked me, "What's that black white thing,
You've hung upon your wall?
It looks like two fish swimming
Within an endless ball.

Or could they be two tadpoles?
One faces up; the other down.
Maybe sperms inside a sphere,
A life form reeling round and round?"

I answered, "It's the tai chi sphere.
It's divided in two parts
One part's heaven; one is earth.
And man lies in its heart.

It is called the yin/yang symbol.
It shows balance in tai chi.
For those who walk the circle
Fear not mortality.

It is an ancient emblem,
For depicting energy
It's about 10,000 things,
It's Chinese philosophy.

For me I see two teardrops.
Of heartbreak and great sorrow.
Our world is full of madness.
And I worry for tomorrow.

The icon pleads for balance,
Claims our lives are much too yang,
There is hate, death, disaster,
There is fighting, loss and pain.

The yin yang in the symbol
Holds the gate to seek the Tao.
It's an easy, peaceful read.
Every chapter shows us how.

It suggests this simple circle,
Shows the cycles of all change,
How nature changes night to day,
How all is re - arranged.

See, things are ever changing,
Yet impossibly they're still.
Long winter ices branches,
Spring warmth will melt the chill.

The tai chi is two equal halves,
One's black; the other's white,
In martial terms the yin/yang
Means withdrawal first; then fight.

The yin/yang's quest is balance
Between poverty and wealth,
Between times of good and evil
Between sickness and in health.

Balance difficult with easy.
We should balance wrong with right.
We must balance hate with love.
Win with softness against might.

The tai chi is Tao's symbol,
That should thwart man's hasty action,
When vengeance and a thirst for war
Become his first reaction.

Revered, my tai chi symbol
Owes its credit to the Asians.
Who discovered that the circle,
Held the key to all creation."

*Authors note: I tried to summarize the theory of tai chi as simply as possible in this poem. Read the Tao Te Ching by Lao Tzu for a complete explanation.

THE YIN YANG

Wuxi

For Sifu Linda Morrissey

I didn't know you
When my words were frozen
Like the cold laundry
Hanging from each apartment.
When my thoughts were scattered
Like snow in a winter paperweight,
Never touching ground.
No, I hadn't met you yet
In this city of concrete,
Colors gray, brown, drab green
Like a New York winter.
Where funny curling shapes
Sprang from the edges
Of rooftops.
Where five AM risers
Held invisible balls
And gracefully moved them with their hands.
Where the unfamiliar skyline,
The chilly river,
And the too many people
Surrounded me in a circle,

And touched my curly hair,
No, I didn't know you then.
That you would be my sage,
Who'd bring East to West,
Who would warm my cold hands,
Teach me the way,
And return to me
My words.

Author's note: The "you" in this poem is Sifu Linda Morrissey. I spent many years learning tai chi from her. She is a natural teacher and one of the kindest people I have known.

TURN AND CHOP WITH FIST

Tai Chi is a Martial Art

I had to share a classroom
With a teacher who was a territorial beast.
She treated me with more contempt
Than if I had been a rat.
She was black and I was white
And her racism was palpable
Like the juice that drips from a rotten tomato.
"Black teachers should teach black students.
No little white mouse like me."
This was her philosophy.

Worse than Cinderella's stepmom,
She insisted I push all the chairs in,
Erase the board, sweep the floor.
I had two minutes to do all these tasks.
She made the list grow more and more.

Stack the books; put the desks in rows,
Find where I misplaced a student's pass,
Ready her throne for her ample ass.
Before she emerged to teach her next class.

The tension built up to new heights,
Until she caught me erasing too late.
This was her moment to start a fight.
I guess to teach me a lesson in hate
She grabbed my left arm and held on tight,

I dropped the eraser,
Turned to face her,
Coiled my right arm under her paw.
Captured her eyes with my laser beam
Then snakily broke her grip with a scream.
Like I was Bruce Lee in a movie scene.

Holding her wrist with a tiger's claw
I stepped behind her; she was strong as a boar.
I placed my left arm across her chest,
And then with a turn of my waist to the left,
I deliberately knocked her to the floor.

Then I turned and ran outside the door.

FAN THROUGH BACK DEMONSTRATED
IN A MARTIAL APPLICATION

On Dragon Hill

(For Bruce La Carrubba)

Smiling through my body
I push the negative energy
Downward into the roots,
Below my feet
Like water seeping into the earth.
My closed eyes imagine my body
Filling with warm yellow sun,
And pulsating energy waves.
Each organ is boosted with
Health and energy.

Smile the spleen,
The liver,
The triple burner,
Smile heart, hands, feet,
Smile with the breath.

Here on Dragon Hill
I find peace
If only for a short time.

My body embraces the yin yang symbol
As I become the tai chi itself.

There is only the sound of the murmuring stream below,
Rippling water over rocks calms the inner spirit.
I feel the shape of water.

Author's note- This poem describes a chi gong meditation. Chi gong consists of exercise
to move healing chi through the meridians of the body.

KICK WITH SOLE WITH STAFF

Return to Readiness

You have a pretty face
Says the Sifu from New York,
At the tai chi camp.
Like any sleep - away camp
Around the world
Where boys hit on girls
And vise versa,
I feel flattered
Like the 16 year old I once was.
Later I see him with his wife.
He dares not make eye contact.

The Sifus are easy to spot
For many are dressed like
Ancient Chinese warriors
Well, yes, some have overdone it,
Like a singer who over-croons.

A man looks like he has arrived
From just crossing the Mojave Desert.
Unshaved, scraggly beard,
Bony; ungroomed long hair

Flowing like the dirty white sheet
He has wrapped himself in.
I wonder what his specialty is…
Jesus disciple?
Volunteer drug addict?
Crazy tai chi uniform inventor,
He is first in line to get punched.

He is obviously at the wrong camp.
He must be a yoga person.

Yes there are crazy tai chi- ers here no doubt.
But I have fun meditating,
Doing san shou
Watching Chen style form
And playing with an invisible ball.
I like the circle walking
Like a dog does before he sits.
One highlight is tracing
The yin yang symbol in 3D
With each body part.
This is how you get loose and coily,
But to those who do not walk the circle,
I look like an inmate from an insane asylum.

There is much beauty here in our shared art,
Passed to us from generations of wise folks.
There is much healing here,
And these refined skills
Take a lifetime to learn.
Thanks to Master Jou,
I will return to these woods.
They are peaceful and the players are fun.
The stream reminds us to "be water, my friends,"*
And a great leader's dream has come true.

Author's note: *popular quote attributed to Bruce Lee

A SNAKE CREEPS

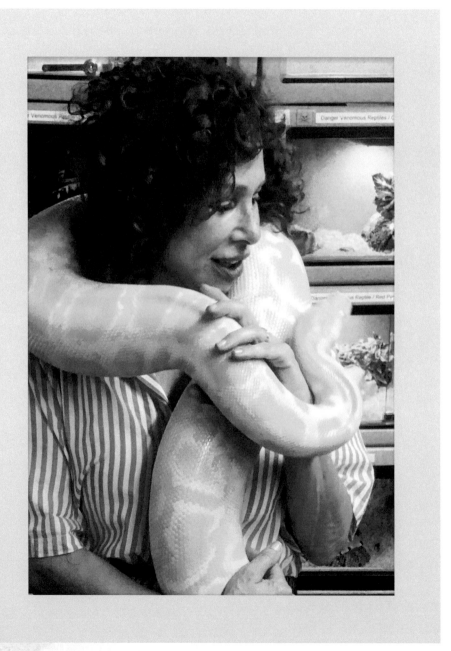

SNAKES CREEP DOWN

ANOTHER SNAKE AT END OF POSTURE

The Anhinga, the Snake Bird

Some think he's a snake
With his serpentine neck,
That like a periscope
Breaks the water's surface.

Ah, like the athlete who's won gold,
On his platform of rock he stands,
Drying his crane-like wings,
Spread widely for admiration.

He struts and peers in each direction
As if to spy some adoration.

The spiky leaves of palm trees
Clap their fronds like fans
In the Florida wind.

*Author's note: The anhinga is familiar to anyone who lives on a pond, canal or stream in Florida. It is a very interesting bird, because it swims with its entire body under the water, People think it's a snake because of its snake-like neck that rotates above the surface. It dive bombs into the water to catch a fish. Then it must dry its wings before it can fly. As the poem says, the anhinga acts like a champion who has won a competition. The postures of tai chi are based on the moves of the crane and the snake, so this bird is a perfect combination of crane and snake.

Seeking Stillness

I'm at the wetlands at Green Cay.
Like a cat I look for movement in the stillness,
Searching for a treasure.
The wind is oddly absent.
Tree limbs do not sway.
The muted sounds are of birds' trilling,
Murmurs of words,
Sneakers on wooden pavement.
I am contentedly alone.
Nothing moves on the bed of pines below me.
There are bubbles on the water's surface,
But I can't see beneath them.
People walk by with expensive cameras
To capture a moment in eternity,
But unable to live in the moment.
A slight breeze suddenly appears
Caressing my face like you once did.
I have emptied my mind of you, seeking calmness.
That is all.
A still white heron stands in the purple pickerel
That roots strongly in the reeds.
Stillness here is safety.
The predator pounces at motion,

Like the eight foot gator I later see,
Lying in the arrowheads, food for ducks.
Can anything be more still than this dragon of death?
His inaction lures his prey.
Little ducks are making lots of noise
And croaking pierces silence.
People are rushing by as if the threat of rain
Is danger.
There is much worse to fear than water.
Three turtles bask quietly on a palm trunk
That extends into the swamp.
Below their shells are black and orange spotted bellies.
Like Halloween candy corn.
Ah, the sun peaks out again,
And the air changes from humidity to coolness.
An older man approaches
To chat me up,
Though I feel unattractive and old,
With my copper curls hidden under a cap,
I am camouflaged and of little interest, I think.
"Have you seen snakes," he asks.
"Yes, one just asked me a question," I reply.
"You're funny," he replies. "Could you meet me
Here on Monday?"

In spite of myself I like him.
But this is not why I am here.
I walk away and find a canopy.
It's a nice place to play tai chi,
Removed, quiet, and sheltered.
People enter anyway
And curiously look at me and the cabbage palm.
They disturb my tranquility like bothersome insects.
As I leave a gusty wind orders
The marsh to move from the stillness into
Frenzied motion
And then everything changes.
Rain falls heavily; peace becomes confusion once more.

Later I discover
I have lost my yin/yang charm.
Did it fall through the wooden slats?
Then the pain returns in my heart.
I remember that I asked you to stay away.

The Two Pools

A toddler laughing with delight,
Splashing chubby fists,
Enjoying the feel and newness of water.
How it drips down his arm,
Stays in his cupped hand,
Runs through the spaces of his fingers.
How hard it feels when he hits the water,
After daddy throws him up,
But under his legs it is so soft.

Children move in the pool like busy bugs,
Throwing water at each other
Like ocean surf hitting the beach.
Dunking and rising with wet dripping hair,
Feeling freedom and blinding
Sunlight upon blue eyes.

Kicks, back floats, goggles,
Eyes open, closed and reddened from chlorine
Rafts, giggles, shouts,
Jumps, twists, turns, flops, whistles, lifeguards,
Sunscreen, freckles, burned shoulders,
Cheeks, legs, blue lips quivering

Bodies shaking,
And mom waiting with an oversized
Soft white fluffy towel
To wrap around the sweetness,
Of the small squirming child who someday may remember
The moment when his mother watched
Every move, jump, stroke, circle
With adoration,
Loving a child more than love itself,
Before she realized that the trouble with time is
It ends.
And one is astonished.

Years later mom is in Florida
Where the pool is filled with gray haired or bald men
Whom she can't tell apart,
And ladies with bellies who
Won't wet their hair
So they hang on Styrofoam noodles,
Moving little, kicking a bit
From knees replaced,
Some are widows, cancer survivors,
The feel of water is common now.
Hats worn to prevent melanomas

On bodies already full of ugly raised brown blotches,
And wrinkled skin falling off bones.
They speak of card games
The portions of food,
Grandchildren,
Pool aerobics in the AM
When wiggling in water once was enough.

The lap pool is empty
Except for the red headed woman,
Who swims alone
But with such smoothness,
The water stays completely still.

CROSS HANDS

Tiger Iris

A stealthy ninja
Sleeps in buds and springs in sun.
Tiger striped flower.

Author's Note: Flowers delight me. My friend has an iris that just amazes me with its gentle fragile beauty, and yet its hint of tiger stripes. The tiger's fierceness vs. the fragile flower is such a perfect example of yin and yang.

AN IRIS AND A TIGER

DEFLECT, PARRY AND PUNCH
AND FIST UNDER ELBOW

SHOOT TIGER WITH BOW

Friendship

I don't have time is what she'll say,
I have many things to do today.
What she is really meaning here,
Is there's no time for you, my dear.

Like rain on the wind - shield of her car,
She'll wipe you away and say au' revoir.

As Lao Tzu said in ancient days,
A Chinese thinker who studied man's ways,
If one cannot find time for you,
He does not have desire to.

Author's note: It is amazing to find such common sense statements from the ancient Chinese philosophers who lived hundreds of years ago. The **I Ching** is a fun book about morality, also called **The Book of Changes** that was written thousands of years ago, full of wisdom and philosophy.

Lesson for the Advanced Tai Chi Practitioner

When you do single whip, watch leg and knee.
Careful when turning; this isn't a dance.
Shift your weight fully; turn your waist right,
Left hand's a mirror; give it a glance.

Have you forgotten the yin and yang rules?
That is your left hand; it's the whip hand you raise.
Always remember which postures to choose.
This art is internal: your skills will amaze.

You play tai chi with invisible tools,
Unlike other sports; you don't see your ball.
Sink your stance; your rear's on a stool,
Pretend it is there, though it isn't at all.

This art's telegraphic to cultivate chi,
It's very complex now to move energy,
Related perhaps to the big bang theory,
Einstein enjoyed its complexity!

SNAKE CREEPS DOWN

Fibromyalgia

It attacks like a tiger,
With deadly force.
Your life as you've known it
Is blasted off course.
You wake up one day,
Like you've caught the flu,
That's clawed inside you,
And split you in two.
Like a stubborn stain.
That never will go.
Its pain is hidden,
Refusing to show,
You feel like an ice cap
That's colder than snow.

Though once you had balance
While living your life.
Like the tai chi symbol,
The black equaled white.

You must say goodbye
To the life you once knew.
Your days without pain
Will be very few.

Treatment

The first step is to try relaxation.
Take yourself to a mountain retreat.
Get plenty of air and lots of good rest.
Make sure it's only veggies you eat.
There are also many medications.
Pain pills probably won't work if you stress,
Maybe some neurological drugs,
And those that help you anti depress.
If these things don't help, try some tai chi,
Or maybe try a gentle swim.
Maybe try a bit of reiki
See a shrink and acupress.

Biofeed and try the gym.
Acupuncture may be the thing,
Or maybe hang and watch TV.

Get massaged; do more tai chi.
Some help may come if you meditate,
But there's really no treatment.
This is your fate.

The life you lived from day to day,
Is finished when fibro steals it away.

Author's Note - I was diagnosed with this nasty disease over thirty years ago. Without tai chi I would probably not be able to move as well as I can. However, doctors are amazed by my flexibility, and commitment to health. The illness has had a deep impact on my life. Even with all the commercials on TV for a certain med to help it, most people have never heard of fibro. It feels like you have the flu without the fever. That is how you live your life. It never goes away.

A lovely pose to lighten the mood: Fair Ladies Work the Shuttles

The Anemone

Upon the coral wall,
Lives the anemone,
Rooting in the reef,
While playing tai chi.

Though her flower is pretty,
Her flowing form free,
She floats in the water,
And strengthens her chi.

An innocent fish
When seeking the flower,
Will never detect
The anemone's power.

When she moves to the right,
She's a toy of the tide.
When she sways to the left
She has something to hide.

She exhales her darts,
With timing and skill.
The anemone offers
Its poison to kill.

A puzzling predator:
Such perfect yang and yin!
She hopes that the clown fish
Will grasp tail and fin.

Her fans are clown fishes,
Who help her to chew,
The waves speak with water
That whispers "Sifu."

The anemone's like
A carnivorous master,
Who balances nature
Preventing disaster.

The anemone
Is a master of the wall.
She isn't a plant.
No, she's not a plant at all.

Note: Those who have taken tai chi will recognize the importance and meaning of the words in the "Anemone." Sifu, of course, is the Chinese word that refers to a master teacher. "Grasping the Bird's Tail" becomes "Grasp tail and fin," in this poem. Yin and yang, duality, the balance of nature, rooting, are other terms found in the study of tai chi.

Poker Face

This morning finds me sick again.
There is a beautiful day outside,
But that is for other people's pleasures.

My head aches; I am as lazy as a very old dog.
Who can't keep up with his master
So I lie on the rug and do nothing.

How did this happen?
Just a few days ago I played tai chi
Among the palm trees.
I twirled within the spiky fronds and punched them
Playfully;
As flecks of foliage landed in my hair
To decorate it.

Now I am too tired to get up.
I am summer one minute,
And a blizzard the next.

I was told I had a disease,
That is a mystery.
I may have a good day, they say,
But this condition will never truly go away.
I hide it well.

I learned long ago as a child,
That bad things happen.
I entered my house after happily playing
In the swamp.
My mother slapped me hard as I came inside,
Innocent and unsuspecting.
I never knew why,
For some questions have no answers.

She left imprints like knife slashes on my face,
Like the paint of an Indian warrior.
I hated her.
And I learned the art of the poker face then.
Now I wear it always.

The Memory of You

Where are you today?
I am balancing on a fallen tree
That's become a bridge for a stream.
I glance behind at my sword,
Careful of keeping my balance,
And trying to lower my stance.
Even the horsefly on my wrist doesn't disturb me,
For I have learned patience.
"Don't you ever stop playing tai chi?" I am asked.
I ignore the pesty bugs
And continue to challenge myself
With my weapon.
The scent of lilac is in the air,
And I remember how you loved them.
I want to find peace
In a world where you no longer exist.
How strange that you are not here.
Where are you today?

Return to Wind

It's late October and the wind has returned,
Colored leaves fall not from trees like autumn in NY,
But rather the wind bends the palm downward,
Like the athlete touching his toes.

I am longing for my friend,
Who has left in the strong gusts,
And my secrets cannot be shared with another.

I no longer know the truth,
Though gentle breezes
Have whispered to my heart for some time now.
Yet still I shake inside
Like a hurricane is,
Trying to uproot me.

I need you more than ever,
My sweet friend,
But you are so far away.

I will practice my tai chi today;
While the wind blows my hair into coils,
That are inside me as well.

Perhaps my postures will sooth me,
And soon I will find you again,
Taste your sweet lips,
And turn sorrow to joy,
In the Florida wind.

I will stand with my back against a strong tree,
With deep roots in the ground,
And dream of your cat like eyes.

HIT TIGERS

Pre-Birth Meditation

Random thoughts flowing
Like water flooding the stream,
Or clouds waving wildly
Pushed by thundering winds.
I chant to be empty.
Nam myoho renge kyo
Nam myoho renge kyo
The sword slashes sometimes,
The snake spits venom,
A fan soothes my sweat.
Nam myoho renge kyo
Nam myoho renge kyo.
There was burning, pain, screams, fear
Nam myoho renge kyo
I beg to remain
I plead to remain.
Nam myoho renge kyo.
You see I remember.
I beg to stay.
I know war. Don't make me leave.
Nam myoho renge kyo.
Sweet kisses, sweet desire

Sweet longing, sweet first kiss.
Disappearing in flames.
Nam myoho renge kyo.
Nam myoho renge kyo.
I tremble. I am an earthquake.
Nam myoho renge kyo.
Nam myoho renge kyo.
Please grant me stillness.
Return me to bliss.

COMMENCEMENT

Camp is for Making Friends

Camp is for making friends,
And this special summer,
My new friend was from China.

I first saw her standing on a rocky ledge,
Her feet tightly attached to the rock,
Like a snail clinging to a boat.
She stared upward at the sky
Like an infant seeing it for the first time.
She seemed enlightened as if she had met the Buddha.
Most people are enchanted by the sparkling lake below,
That shown with a million diamonds from the sun,
But it was the sky that held her attention.

"In my country the sky is gray," she later told me.
It is always covered with hazy clouds.
The sky here matches your blue eyes," she said.

I taught her to love the feel of the lake.
To enjoy its coolness on a hot day.
First, she only put her tiny toes in,
But later she splashed with her arms and legs

Like the birds who came to fish.
She even dunked her entire head
And compared it to rain on her face.

She taught me to use chopsticks,
To eat Chinese food that I had never tried,
To drink tea, and appreciate all the soda
We could buy.
She loved our American food, our burgers and fries,
And most of all, ice cream. Bing qi lin.
She told me about her chaperone
Who looked like a crane
When he played tai chi each morning.

She loved to wake before dawn to see the sunrise,
And to draw the colors of the sunset.

She giggled at my curly hair that she pulled.
It was a head of snakes she told me.
I loved her small figure and gracefulness,
And her eyes that angled upwards like an accent mark.
When she slept over at my house,
She thought it was a castle.
"There are so many trees here," she said,

"But not as many beautiful gardens as in China."

She was surprised at how many clothes I had,
And how many toys my brother owned.
She wore only two different outfits.
She kept room in her suitcase for all the gifts
She would bring home to her family near Beijing.

She saw many animals at the camp.
There were deer with spotted fawns
Following behind.
Huge hawks, wild turkeys, and eagles were seen,
And cardinals as red as a Chinese wedding dress.
Raccoons sometimes arrived late in the day
Who had been hiding in the bushes.
They were like a cleanup crew after lunch.

She wanted to attend college here in the States.
"We will go together my friend," she said.

I cried the day she flew back home.

ROLL BACK AND RAISE HANDS

DEMONSTRATION OF SHOULDER STROKE

For Love of Water

5 Haikus

Fall from a full cloud.
We are raindrops in the night,
Piercing a dark sea.

Whirling winds and waves
Toss us up, down, around, back:
Grasping the bird's tail.

You balance on top.
Currents push me down below.
Then I rise: you fall.

We are the tide's toys.
Joined together as one.
Swept and swayed apart.

Swim to my center.
We are two halves of a whole.
You, love, complete me.

Prayer to Buddha

Buddha claimed that the trouble with time
Is you think you have it.
Even she thought she had time with her soldier.
To kiss him deeply and long.
To feel him close to her.
To feel his arms around her,
And do nothing but breathe.

When he left in silence,
When he showed his unwillingness to flow beside her,
The cold Shanghai winds were warmer
Than his callous retreat.
She told him, "Thank you.
For ending our time."

Just as war always follows peace,
Apathy always follows passion.
And sadness always follows joy.
Always.
She knew this to be true.

And yet alone she still felt longing,
That continued to threaten like the Yangtze River,

Blocked by the Three Gorges Dam.
"How sad is my life," she thought.
"Oh Buddha, perhaps I have too much time!"

DEFLECT, PARRY AND PUNCH

Dreaming the Palms of Bagua

Walking a circle I am graceful as a doe.
My steps are carefully placed.
You are here as well, behind me, in front, side to side.
Together we bend and sway in harmony.
We love without touch.
The mystery in this dance is that
It is not a dance at all.
It is the play of the praying mantis
Who may devour her lover.
It is the walk of bagua,
Where I close and open like a flower.

I am powerful, free,
Like a bud who blossoms
Spreading into full glory in the sun.
Or a woman who secretly carries
Life to burst forth.
I can change my palms,
And seduce you like Medusa,
My coiling curls are serpents,
A blue eyed snake in the Garden of Eden.

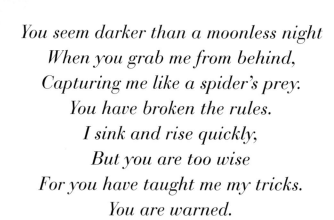

You seem darker than a moonless night
When you grab me from behind,
Capturing me like a spider's prey.
You have broken the rules.
I sink and rise quickly,
But you are too wise
For you have taught me my tricks.
You are warned.

Down we go and my only recourse
Is to grab and pull what I must
To escape.
I could hurt you.

Perhaps you should not risk your presence in my circle,
But here there is no right or wrong.
This is my addiction.
Should you match my changes,
Resistance softens.

Author's note: This poem attempts to describe the complex tai chi form of Bagua. It is absolutely amazing to watch, and is quite advanced. Unfortunately for me I stopped practicing it long ago, and I have regretted it.

Seven Stars

My legs form circles round his waist,
Our lips together, hands entwined,
I'm dreaming on this summer night.
That I am his and he is mine.
I think I'm travelling to Bliss.
I feel his essence joined to me.
I think perhaps he feels the same.
The chemistry; the energy.
His spirit permeates my soul.
I wish that time would stop right here.
And then I feel a nameless force,
That lifts us both into the air.
So combined in love are we,
I can't tell which is he or me.
There is no sense of gravity.

We are the tai chi sphere in space.
We're yin in yang, and yang in yin.
Transformed by what I can't explain, He is me and I am him.

Desire pushes faster now,
The planet earth is very far.
A nameless force spins us around
And changes us to seven stars.
So if you look at night time's sky,
You'll see us blinking with our light,
A constellation made from love,
The universe is ours tonight.

*Author's note: Love must be the ruling force of the universe if mankind is to continue to exist. Seven Stars is one of the 37 tai chi postures.

SEVEN STARS

The Elements

The wooden dock is wobbly
As I'm practicing my form.
Rough waves from underneath
Roil from yesterday's storm.

But as long as it takes me,
I'll stay here and try,
To wave hands like clouds,
Floating white through the sky.

The cold air's like steel,
Though the autumn sun's bright.
The moon's stubborn face,
Persists in the light.

And yet I must practice,
What I've set out to do,
And learn from the truths
That the old masters knew.

From the sight of their mountain,
The earth, lake, and trees,
The masters created
And performed their tai chi.

And though you're in the cabin,
Warm and waiting for me,
Maybe building a fire,
Perhaps brewing green tea.

I still play on the dock,
Filling with chi,
Though you're in the cabin
Waiting for me.

*Author's note- This is one of my Romantic-Philosophy poems. The five elements that are important to Chinese philosophy are found in this poem: wood, fire, metal, water, earth.

PRESS

My First Friend

Learning of your death from a facebook post,
Blasted my chi into unrestrained flames.
You were my first best friend,
Our lives a circle of countless hellos and goodbyes
That continued through childhood's special love.
Alone now, I sit on a ground of pine needles,
Where I've practiced tai chi.

This park reminds me of you.
For mysteries surround me like the ones we explored
As children.
Rocks, bugs, lizards, birds, curious metal objects, toads, coins,
Leaves and water.
Always water.

Rainy days were toy soldier war games,
Movies, TV, hiding in the closet.
You gave me a princess figurine,
For I was too girly for rifles and bayonets.

Memories shake me into sobs of loss.
I will never again see your Dutch blue eyes,

Your new photos,
Your funny replies to my posts.
I try to calm my chi through stillness,
But I am not ready to let you go.
I am not ready:

BRUSH KNEE

SINGLE WHIP

Part the Wild Horse's Mane

The horses in the sketch are stampeding with fright,
Like a crowd of people who have heard an explosion.
Their bright green color belies their frenzied action,
For is green not the color of relaxation?
Of course, the artist is Chinese and knows the concept of Yin and Yang.

The morning grass is a blanket of green sprinkled with daisies.
The thick leaves of trees are a green umbrella for an afternoon of rest.
This is where I sit now away from the sketch above my bed.

Once I sat here with you beneath a shady tree,
And the world sparkled with green and blue-
I leaned over and kissed your lips,
And your eyes opened wide with surprise.

PART THE WILD HORSE'S MANE
OR SLANTINGLY FLYING

Sonnet to Bruce Lee

Greatest Asian warrior, Li Xiao Long,
Known in the States as the actor Bruce Lee,
Little Dragon, your memory stays strong,
Locked in our hearts and within history.

Great Chinese warrior, unmatched in deed,
Like Achilles, you shared a fatal flaw.
So fast, the film lens could not catch your speed.
Your short stay on earth struck us with awe.

Philosopher, poet, nationalist,
Your skin your own armor screaming, "hah woo!"
From one inch away, wood split from your fist.
Your exemplary goal was to share Kung-fu.

On Wudang Mountain the rushing water falls,
Guarding the soul of one fastest of all.

Printed in the United States
By Bookmasters